OUR GRANDFATHERS' FLIES

Tying Flies with Furs, Feathers, and Hair

DAVID L. MCELWAIN

Cover by Seth Bourdman
Edited by Lauren S. Demuth
Photography by Amy Shalz

PUBLISHED BY TROUT BUM PRESS, LLC

2012 © All rights reserved. No part of this book may be reproduced without expressed permission of the publisher except in the case of brief excerpts in critical reviews and articles. All inquiries should be addressed to:

Trout Bum Press, LLC
940 Plum Creek Parkway, suite 104
Castle Rock, CO 80104
flies@troutbumpress.com

ISBN: 0615617808
ISBN-13: 9780615617800

DEDICATION

To: Lauren Demuth for all your help, involvement, and support making this book happen. Without your encouragement, the pile of printouts, notes, and scribbling would still be sitting on my desk.

Contents

Acknowledgement i
Forward ii
Section I Dry Flies 1
    Fire Hole 2
    Bi-Visible 4
    Grey Fox 6
    Anolomink 8
    Banks Fly 10
    Barber Pole 12
    Beaverkill II 14
    Black Gnat Special 16
    Blue Quill 18
    Whitchurch Dun 20
    Beaverkill (original) 22
    Quill Gordon 24
    Quill Gordon Dark 26
    Atherton #1 30
    Atherton #6 32
    The Adams 34
    H&L Variant 36
    Royal Wulff 38

Section II Wet Flies 41
    Yellow Grey Hackle 42
    Bird's Stone Nymph 44
    Breadcrust Nymph 46

Blades' Olive Nymph 48
Black Gnat Nymph 50
Beaverkill Nymph 52
Female Beaverkill Nymph 54
Atherton Light Nymph 56
Atherton Dark Nymph 58
Atherton #1 Wet Fly 60
Carrot Nymph 62
Gray Ghost 64
Mormon Girl 66
Sofa Pillow 68
Wooly Worm 70
Author's Biography 73
Bibliography 75

Acknowledgements

The list of supporters and contributors to my knowledge and craft is quite substantial. Each one shared their wisdom and talent, and for that, I am forever grateful.

Char Bloom   Jim Boden   Seth Bourdman

Tim Daughton   Matt Dill   Steve Fritz   Gene Goddard

Ryan Gunnel   Simone Geoffrion   Blaine Haskell

Zac Hill   Chris Hosmer   Mike Huffman

Lefty Krey   Bill Louthan   John L. Morris   Al Noraker

Frank Prekel   **Charlie Reading**   Jerry Rogers

Alan Reyes   Grant Rollo

FORWARD

I have been preparing for this book for a couple of decades. I collected articles, stories, and flies until there was no more room to collect. What fascinates me is where and when did the actual sport come from. What is the history of the sport, where did it begin. Logistically, how did it get to North America and to me,

In this book I share the route fly fishing traveled across the pond from 1850 to 1950. There were unique travelers and interesting forms of transportation. They encountered a myriad of problems. They addressed them, solved them and moved forward.

All of this was transpiring while America dealt with The Civil War, World War I and World War II, not to mention The Industrial Revolution. Still through it all, the communication continued and the information transferred. The entomologists collected their specimens and the tiers transformed them into patterns. The streams ran and the fish spawned.

I selected the flies and their creators that spanned these one hundred years because were it not for their passion and entrepreneurial spirit, fly fishing, as we know it today, may not have developed.

Section One: Dry Flies

Our Grandfathers' Flies

Fire Hole

Originator: Ray Bergman
1930s
Recipe:
Hook: Mustad 94840 or equivalent dry fly hook size 10-20
Thread: Black 8/0 (6/0 builds to heavy on the eye of this fly)
Wing: Woodduck flank fibers
Tail : Woodduck flank fibers
Body: Cream fur dubbing (seal fur dubbing may also be used)
Hackle: one each black and grizzly

DAVID L. MCELWAIN

FIRE HOLE

Step 1. Attach the thread to the hook and tie in a section of Woodduck flank fibers.
Step 2. Dub an even amount of cream fur dubbing on about 3 inches of thread, then wrap forward creating a body. (creating the body by tightening with fingertips)
Step 3. Tie in and evenly divide the Woodduck flank, to create the wings
Step 4. Tie in one black and one grizzly hackle and palmer forward four times behind the wings and four in front of the wings and whip finish

Ray Bergman created this fly while fishing the Fire Hole in Yellowstone. Initially he thought it was good in the smaller size but soon discovered success in the larger sizes as well. Bergman, along with many fly fishers from the east eventually succumbed to the stories of the trout bounty in Montana, Idaho, and Wyoming and set off to investigate.

Bergman was a prolific fly-tier and writer. He was the author of outdoor living and fishing articles for "Field and Stream", "Outdoor Life", and Hunting and Fishing". In 1932, he published "Just Fishing" and opened his own business "Ray Bergman Angling Specialties" and began tying flies commercially. In 1938, he wrote one of the greatest books in angling history, the classic "Trout" in which he published over 500 wet fly patterns. The truth be known, Ray Bergman liked to fish the dry fly best.

Our Grandfathers' Flies

Bi-Visible

Originator: Edward Ringwood Hewitt
circa 1926
Recipe:
Hook: The hook should be a 20 to size 12 dry fly hook
(recommendation 94840 Mustad)
Thread: Black 6/0
Hackle: Brown (rear)
Hackle: White (front)

David L. McElwain

Bi-Visible

Step 1. Attach the thread and then double cover the hook with thread to the bend of hook.
Step 2. Tie in one brown hackle and palmer forward to the 80% point of hook.
Step 3. Tie in the white hackle palmer 4 times and tie off.
Step 4. Make a head and whip finish

Over the decades Bi-Visibles have been tied in many color combinations, representing emerging flies from midge to May flies and Caddis. The Bi-Visible dates back to 1926 when Charles Merrill added the white hackle to the front of the fly.

Charles Hewitt expressed his review of the Bi-Visible in an article "Telling on the Trout", 1926. "Dark colors are more visible to the trout from below than light colors and, therefore, take more fish under most conditions and are more generally used. They are often more difficult to see on the water than the light flies. This is the reason for my favorite design of fly which I call the Bi-Visible. The Bi-Visible consists of a palmer-tied brown hackle on the head of which is wound a small wisp of white hackle."

This pattern is still used today. Other patterns that were derived from this tying style are the Renegade and the Griffith Gnat.

OUR GRANDFATHERS' FLIES

THE GREY FOX

Originator: Preston Jennings
circa 1930s
Recipe:
Hook: Number 12 dry fly
Thread: Silk primrose
Tail: Ginger cock's barbs
Body: Light fawn colored fur from a red fox
Hackle: Light grizzly and light ginger
Wing: Flank feather of a Mallard drake

David L. McElwain

The Grey Fox

Step 1. Attach the thread to the hook and advance to the bend of the hook
Step 2. Tie in a section of the ginger hackle barbs
Step 3. Dub about 3" of thread with the fox fur
Step 4. Wrap forward forming body (tighten dubbing with fingertips)
Step 5. Attach one grizzly hackle and ginger hackle
Step 6. Palmer the grizzly hackle over the ginger
Step 7. Whip finish

This fly is a classic eastern imitation of the Stenonema Fuscum, also known as the Grey Fox. This fly is similar to the March Brown and the Heptagenia. They are both large May flies and are lightly shaded flies and subtle attractors.

The a Virginia native, Preston Jennings, was a legend in the eastern Catskills. He attended the Medical College of Virginia and proceeded to set the standard of excellence, with his study of fly-fishing entomology, to which all subsequent work on the topic is measured.

His study of light refraction off an insect on the surface and how it is perceived by the trout below was the basis of his fly patterns – "The American March Brown and the Grey Fox". His work ,"A Book of Trout Flies", published in 1935, completed Louis Rhead's work by producing the reference and classification of " American Trout Stream Insects.

ANOLOMINK

Originator – W.C. Dette
catalogue 1935
Recipe:
Hook: Standard straight eye dry fly
Body: Black dry dubbing
Ribbing: Orange floss or heavy thread
Hackle: White badger
Wings: Black hackle tied spent
Thread: Black 8/0

David L. McElwain

Anolomink

Step 1. Attach thread to hook and tie in a length of orange floss
Step 2. Dub about 3 inches of thread and advance to just past half way of hook – leaving room to add wings and hackle
Step 3. Form body by tightening dubbing with fingertips
Step 4. Segment body with orange floss forward to front of body
Step 5. Tie in badger hackle and lay back
Step 6. Select and tie in two black hackle tips, figure 8 to hold in spent position
Step 7. Palmer hackle with 4 wraps behind and in front of wings. Tie off and whip finish leaving small head

Walt and Winnie Dette owned and operated "W C Dette Dry Flies", in Roscoe, New York. They established their business in 1927 and regularly issued catalogues containing over 100 flies that they tied themselves. Walt, was remembered as one of the best tiers that the Catskill School, ever produced. He designed and adapted many dry, wet, and streamer patterns that are still used today. The Conover, Dette Special, Walt's Dace, Dette Caddis, Coffin Fly, and the Green Drake Mayfly Spinner to name a few. Their business is still operated today by their daughter Mary Dette Clark.

BANKS FLY

Originator- W.C. Dette
catalogue 1935
Recipe:
Hook: Standard dry fly
Body: Grey red mixed dubbing
Tail: Ginger hackle barbules
Hackle: Ginger and blue grey (blue dun)
Wings: Blue-grey hackle point (tips) (blue dun)
Thread: Grey

DAVID L. MCELWAIN

BANKS FLY

Step 1. Attach thread to hook and tie in a fair amount of ginger hackle barbules to make tail.

Step 2. Mix with fingers a good amount of red and grey dry dubbing.

Step 3. Dub a 3" or so length of thread and wrap forward to form body, tighten with fingers to even shape.

Step 4. Select hackle with one dun and one ginger matched hackles with palmering 4 times behind wings and 4 times in front of wings – tie off and whip finish.

OUR GRANDFATHERS' FLIES

BARBER POLE

Originator – W.C. Dette
catalogue 1935
Recipe:
hook: Standard Dry Fly
Thread: Tan
Body: Black dry dubbing
Tail: Tan speckled (Partridge)
Ribbing: Red floss
Wings: Tan speckled (Partridge)
Hackle: Blue-grey (blue dun)
Note: a small drop of hood cement will help stabilize wings

David L. McElwain

Barber Pole

Step 1. Attach thread to hook and tie in several Partridge tail feather barbules.

Step 2. Tie in a length of red floss.

Step 3. Dub about 3" of thread and wrap forward creating body.

Step 4. Select two Partridge wing feather tips and tie in and position in upright position.

Step 5. Select two blue dun hackles, tie in and palmer forward 4 times in back of wings and 4 times in front of wings – tie off and whip finish.

Our Grandfathers' Flies

Beaverkill II

Originator – W.C. Dette
catalogue 1935
Recipe:
Hook: Standard Dry Fly
Body: White dubbing
Tail: Brown hackle barbules
Hackle: Brown dry fly hackles
Wings: Grey hackle tips
Thread: Grey dun 8/0

DAVID L. MCELWAIN

BEAVERKILL II

Step 1. Attach thread to hook at midpoint and wrap to bend in hook.

Step 2. Select a generous amount of brown hackle barbules and tie in for tail.

Step 3. Dub a 3 inch or so length of thread to form body and wrap forward to halfway point and tie off. Tighten the dubbing with fingertips to smooth body.

Step 4. Tie in a pair of grey hackle tips and adjust to length of hook shank and bring upright.

Step 5. Tie in the dry fly hackle and palmer upright 4 times behind and in front of wings. Tie off and whip finish.

Our Grandfathers' Flies

Black Gnat Special

Originator – W.C. Dette
catalogue 1935
Recipe:
Hook: Standard Dry Fly
Body: Black dubbing
Tail: Grey speckled barbules from Partridge
Hackle: Black
Wings: Grey speckled hackle tips from Partridge
Thread: Rusty dun 8/0

David L. McElwain

Black Gnat Special

Step 1. Attach thread to hook at forward part in front on midsection 60% forward.

Step 2. Tie in generous amount of Partridge barbules for tail

Step 3. Dub a 3" or so section of thread generously and advance dubbing to form the body and tighten with fingertips.

Step 4. Tie in a hackle and lay back.

Step 5. Select a matched pair of Partridge tips for wings and tie them in and separate.

Step 6. Palmer hackle 4 times in back of wings and 4 times in front of wing, then whip finish.

Blue Quill

Originator: W.C. Dette
catalogue 1935
Recipe:
Hook: Standard Dry Fly
Body: Stripped Peacock herl quill
Tail: Blue-grey hackle barbules
Hackle: Blue-grey hackle
Wings: Blue-grey hackle tips

BLUE QUILL

Step 1. Attach thread to hook and advance to bend of hook and tie in a generous amount of hackle barbules for tail.
Step 2. Tie in quill and palmer to front forming body
Step 3. Tie in a matched pair of hackle tips for wings and separate
Step 4. Tie in and palmer forward the hackle 4 times in back and in front of wings.
Step 5. Whip finish.

Note: Palmering a second hackle will add more stability to this fly since the quill doesn't offer much in the way of support.

OUR GRANDFATHERS' FLIES

WHITCHURCH DUN

Originator: W. C. Dette
catalogue 1935
Recipe:
Body: Yellow floss or dubbing or heavy yellow thread
Tail: Ginger hackle barbules
Hackle: Ginger
Wing: Grey or dun wing
Thread: Rusty dun
Hook: 10-20

DAVID L. McELWAIN

WHITCHURCH DUN

Step 1. Attach thread to hook.

Step 2. Tie in a generous amount of hackle barbules.

Step 3. Tie in yellow thread, floss, and dubbing to create body.

Step 4. Match a pair of hackle tips for the wings and tie in.

Step 5. Tie in hackle and palmer forward 4 times in back of the wings and 4 times in front of wings.

Step 6. Whip finish head.

BEAVERKILL

(original)

Originator: Harry Pritchard
circa 1850
Recipe:
Hook: 94840 or equivalent dry hook
Wing: Slate grey quill, double divided
Tail: Woodduck flank fibers
Body: White floss
Hackle: Brown palmered

Though many tiers from 1880 through late 30s and 40s have tied versions of this fly, both dry and wet, it is believed that this is the original version of its dry form.

DAVID L. MCELWAIN

BEAVERKILL
(original)

Step 1. Attach thread to hook and advance to bend of hook and tie in a generous amount of Wood Duck flank barbules.
Step 2. Tie in, by the tip and lay back.
Step 3. Tie in a length of floss and advance forward creating the body.
Step 4. Tie in and upright a pair of quills divided.
Step 5. Palmer hackle sparsely to wing, then palmer close 4 times behind and 4 times in front of wing.
Step 6. Whip finish.

There seems to be some confusion regarding who tied the original Beaverkill! The story goes "an English pattern was furnished to Harry Pritchard by Judge James Fitch. It is believed that the English pattern copied was the Silver Sedge."

Our Grandfathers' Flies

Quill Gordon

Originator: Theodore Gordon
1854-1915
Hook: Standard nymph hook 29-10
Thread: Dun or grey (8/0 rusty dun UNI-thread is a great fit)
Tail: Medium dun hackle barbules
Body: Peacock quill from eye feather, reinforced with gold thread
Wings: Woodduck flank, tied upright and divided
Hackle: Medium rusty dun cock hackle

DAVID L. MCELWAIN

QUILL GORDON

Step 1. Attach thread to hook and advance to bend of hook.

Step 2. Tie in a section of hackle barbules for tail.

Step 3. Select a quill section from the eye of as Peacock feather and strip and flatten with a white eraser, tie in wire and quill.

Step 4. Wrap quill forward creating body.

Step 5. Reverse wrap gold wire over quill.

Step 6. Tie in hackle and lay back.

Step 7. Select a fair amount of Woodduck flank and measure to length of hook shank, tie in forward over hook eye, raise and divide.

Step 8. Palmer the hackle forward 4 times in back of wings and 4 times in front of wings, tie off and whip finish.

Our Grandfathers' Flies

Quill Gordon Dark

Originator: Theodore Gordon
1854-1915
Recipe:
Wings: Bronze Mallard
Tail: Woodduck flank barbules
Body: Stripped Peacock herl quill
hackle: Dark rusty dun cock hackle
Note: Thread and hook will be the original Quill Gordon. The stripped quill of a Peacock quill is used instead of a quill from the eye feather.

David L. McElwain

Theodore Gordon (1854-1915) A native of Pittsburg, PA; he fished the limestone creeks near Carisle. Gordon was a fly fisher and fly tier and ultimately the creator of the Quill Gordon. He settled in the hamlet of Beaverkill, NY. He corresponded with friends and tiers in England in an effort to develop flies that could endure the faster currents of the American mountain streams.

Our Grandfathers' Flies

35 Inverness Terrace
Hyde Park W
February 22, 1890
Dear Sir:

You must excuse my delay in replying to your favour of 15th ult.

I can quite imagine that in some parts of your country fish could be taken with dry fly where more usual sunk fly would be of no avail- my difficulty however as to advising you of patterns likely to be successful is chiefly due to the fact that I have no knowledge of the streams or lakes nor of the genera and species of natural fly prevalent in them-hence I have thought it better to send you a few of the flies I use myself as patterns rather than order here what might prove after all useless to you-knowing your own rivers you can then select the patterns which seem likely and dress them yourself or order in the U.S.- if you prefer to have them dressed here and want my advise as to the best dresser I should recommend you giving your order to Mr. G. Holland-Bridge Street-Salisbury. If you tell him that the patterns were dressed for and by me and give the name he would be able to send you exactly what you wanted-in all cases however give him the size of hook and to assist you in this I have enclosed a set of the original size from 000 to 4 (Edit-English system) The shape of the hooks not made by Hutchinson are to my mind an improvement on the original one as designed by my friend Mr. Hall-being more of hackle only.

If you should be unsuccessful with the floating flies or in doubt as to patterns please try and collect a few of the natural insects in spirit and send them to me by post and if I can dress imitations I will-a tube 3"x 1" corked, quite full of methylated spirit packed with cotton wool in a small block of wood bored out to receive the tube will travel all over the world by post- of course the color does fade to a certain degree and even in spirit but from experience I think I could allow for this and possibly even might know the genera and species-

If I can be of any further assistance to you pray write and in any case kindly let me know the result of your experiments-

With kind regards,
Yours faithfully

Frederick M. Halford

Theodore Gordon, Esq.
From "The Complete Fly Fisherman: The notes and letters of Theodore Gordon" edited by John McDonald. Pub. By Charles Scribner's Sons 1947- Image hosted on www.classictrout.com

David L. McElwain

As a result of Gordon's correspondence with Halford , American fly fishing would be forever changed. He ultimately received 50 dry flies from the English dry fly enthusiast. Gordon adapted the patterns by using a stiffer hackle, divided upright wings, and changed some colors . These changes resulted in flies that mimicked the local entomology that could survive in the faster steams like the Battenkill.

John McDonald compiled Gordon's articles, notes and letters. "The complete Fly Fisherman: The Notes and Letters of Theodore Gordon" was published in 1947.

ATHERTON #1

Dry Fly

Originator: John Atherton
circa 1951
Hook: 12-16 dry fly
Thread: Brown or cream
Tail: Pale dun hackle barbules
Body: Pale cream fox belly fur
Ribbing: Small oval gold tinsel
Hackle: Light cream or pale ginger and one light grizzly hackle
Wing: Hackle points from a light, glassy natural dun

DAVID L. MCELWAIN

ATHERTON #1
Dry Fly

Step 1. Attach thread to hook and advance to bend of hook
Step 2. Select a section of hackle barbules and tie in for tail in front of bend.
Step 3. Tie in tinsel for ribbing and lay back.
Step 4. Dub 3" or so of thread with fox fur and dub the hook from the body.
Step 5. Reverse rib with tinsel.
Step 6. Tie in hackle and lay back.
Step 7. Tie in hackle points for wing and raise and separate.
Step 8. Palmer pale ginger hackle 4 times in back and 4 times in front of wing, palmer the grizzly over the ginger 4 times in back and 4 times in front of wing.

Born in Brainard, Minnesota, John Atherton was an artist whose works were displayed in fine galleries around the world. Like Preston Jennings, Atherton was fascinated by the light and color and its effects on the behavior of trout. His findings were published in the classic "The Fly and The Fish", 1951. He was buried along the banks of his favorite river, the Battenkill, in Vermont.

ATHERTON #6

Dry Fly

Originator: John Atherton
circa 1951
Recipe:
Thread: 8/0 dun or rusty dun
Hook: Standard dry fly
Tail: Dark Rusty dun hackle barbules
Body: Mixture of dark muskrat or mole and some red-brown seal fur – to create a body of brownish gray color
Ribbing: oval gold tinsel
Wing: This wing can be varied somewhat but Atherton's preference was Bali duck side feather, bronze Mallard and dark Mandarin
Hackle: Rusty dun

DAVID L. MCELWAIN

ATHERTON #6
Dry Fly

Step 1. Attach thread to hook and advance to bend of hook.

Step 2. Select a group of hackle barbules, measure to length of hook and tie in.

Step 3. Tie in a length of gold tinsel and lay back

Step 4. Select and mix, in coffee grinder, the dubbing. Then dub a 3" section of thread and wind forward to form body.

Step 5. Reverse wrap forward segmenting body.

Step 6. Tie in hackle and lay back.

Step 7. Tie in a selection of barbules from selected feathers, raise and separate.

Step 8. Palmer 4 times back and front of wings, whip finish.

OUR GRANDFATHERS' FLIES

THE ADAMS

Originator: Lenard Hallady
circa 1922
Recipe:
Hook: Mustad 94840 or 94833, Orvis Supreme or any standard dry fly hook 20-8
Thread: Black – silk, monochord or nylon (8/0 UNI-thread)
Tail: Two strands from a Golden Pheasant neck feather
Hackle: Mixed from neck feathers of Barred Plymouth Rock and Rhode Island Red roosters
Wings: Narrow neck feathers of Barred Plymouth Rock rooster, tied "advanced" forward and in a semi-spent manner
Body: Soft grey dubbing fur, muskrat fur

Note: Over the years The Adams has under gone many changes, creating quite an interesting family of flies from a female version to loop wing version. Parachute version, Spinner version, Irresistible version, etc., and is still today, as in the beginning, one of the most versatile dry flies you can find in any local fly shop. It blends well into any hatch from May flies to Caddis and small stone flies.

DAVID L. MCELWAIN

THE ADAMS

Step 1. Attach thread to hook and advance to bend of hook and tie in Pheasant hackle.
Step 2. Dub a 3" or so length of thread and wind forward to center of hook.
Step 3. Tie in and lay back the two hackles.
Step 4. Select and tie in a matched pair of hackle tips.
Step 5. Palmer each hackle forward 4 times behind and 4 times in front of wings. Allow wings to slant forward slightly toward eye of hook, whip finish.

Leonard Hallady was born in 1872. He spent the next 60 years living on the banks of the Boardman River. He gave a freshly tied fly to Mr. Adams to try it out one day. When Adams returned he said it was a "knockout", Hallady named it "The Adams" because "he made the first good catch on it". Hallady also tied the Hair Stone.

Our Grandfathers' Flies

H & L Variant

Originator: Dr. William Baigent
circa 1875
Recipe:
Hook: Standard dry hook
Thread: Brown
Tail: Calf tail or body hair
Body: Stripped Peacock herl quill, followed by a thick herl
Hackle: Brown – oversized x2
Wing: Calf tail or body hair

H & L Variant

Step 1. Attach thread and hook and advance to bend of hook and attach a generous bunch of calf tail

Step 2. Strip 2-3 Peacock herl quill and wrap forward ¼ length of hook and tie in 2-3 Peacock herl and wrap thickly to mid way point of hook

Step 3. Tie in hackle and lay back.

(Note: Variants were tied with twice the normal hackle length.)

Step 4. Tie in a generous amount of calf tail.

Step 5. Set upward and separate for wing.

Step 6. Palmer hackle forward 4 times in back of wings and 4 times in front of wings, tie off and whip finish.

Dr. William Baigent of Yorkshire, England, is said to be one of England's most successful anglers. His patterns were all dressed with "natural old English game cock feathers". The long hackles gave buoyancy and made them ride higher. The doctor also registered a set of twelve patterns as "Refracta Dry Flies". He had separated the hackles, short were used as legs, and long, for their floating qualities. Today, we refer to long as saddle hackles and the shorter as cape hackles.

ROYAL WULFF

Originator: Lee Wulff
circa 1930s
Recipe:
Hook: Dry fly up eye
Thread: Black 8/0
Tail: Dark deer hair
Body: Green Peacock herl with red floss in center
Hackle: Dark brown cock hackle
Wings: White buck tail, tied upright and divided

DAVID L. McELWAIN

ROYAL WULFF

Step 1. Attach thread to hook and advance to bend of hoot and tie in the deer hair for tail.
Step 2. Tie in 2 Peacock herl and palmer ¼ length of hook, tie in red floss and wrap 1/8" area, tie in 2 more strands of Peacock herl and palmer to ½ way point of hook.
Step 3. Tie in hackle and lay back.
Step 4. Palmer hackle 4 times in back of wings and 4 times in front of wings, whip finish.

Lee Wulff was a native of Valdez, Alaska, and he was a founding member of The Federation of Fly Fishers and Theodore Gordon Fly Fishers. He was a pilot, artist, and film maker; but he had a passion for the Atlantic Salmon fishery. In the 1930s, he developed his famous dry flies known as The Wulff series. The Wulff School, which stands today on the banks of the Beaverkill river was, established by he and his wife, Joan Salvato-Wulff, in 1979 and is still in operation today.
Lee's most famous quote "A game fish is too valuable a resource to be caught only once." Many believe he was the father of catch and release fishing.

Section Two : Wet Flies

Our Grandfathers' Flies

Yellow Grey Hackle

Originator: unknown
First established 1910
Recipe:
Hook: Scud Hook
Thread: Black 8/0
Hackle: Grey grizzly
Body: Yellow wool or fur dubbing
Ribbing: gold tinsel

David L. McElwain

Yellow Grey Hackle

Step 1. Place hook in vice, attach thread, and secure a length of gold French tinsel.
Step 2. Dub 2 ½ to 3" thread.
Step 3. Advance the dubbing forward, creating the body. Tighten body with fingertips.
Step 4. Reverse wrap the gold tinsel to the front of the body and secure.
Step 5. Tie in a grey grizzly hackle and palmer forward two times, splaying back between palmers and secure and whip finish.

This fly can be tied in many sizes, it can be used for trout and pan fish alike. It is a wet fly and usually used as a dropper. Generally fished in a dead drift so to represent a rising emerger.

Our Grandfathers' Flies

Bird's Stone Nymph

Originator: Cal Bird of Reno, Nevada
circa 1950s
Recipe:
Hook: 3XL heavy wire
Thread: Orange or yellow
Tails: Dyed brown biots
Body: Brown dubbing, # 15 or 20 lead wire
Ribbing: Orange or yellow floss
Wing case: Dark brown mottled quill (turkey)
Thorax: Peacock herl
Hackle: Brown or furnace

David L. McElwain

Bird's Stone Nymph

Step 1. Attach the thread to the hook and advance to the bend of the hook.
Step 2. Tie in the biots one on each side of hook.
Step 3. Tie in a length of 4 strand floss.
Step 4. Tie in at center of hook lead wire and wrap 6 to 8 times toward eye of hook, cover with thread.
Step 5. Return thread to bend of hook and dub 4 to 5 inches of thread with dubbing and wrap forward covering lead and creating body.
Step 6. Reverse wrap the floss over dubbed body.
Step 7. Tie in a piece of turkey quill about ¼" wide.
Step 8. Tie in furnace hackle.
Step 9. Tie in several strands of Peacock herl.
Step 10. Wrap Peacock her forward and tie off.
Step 11. Palmer hackle forward and tie off.
Step 12. Lay turkey quill over the top pushing hackle down.
Step 13. Tie off, whip finish and lacquer head and wing case.

This was a ground- breaking stone fly nymph. At the time of its' introduction, it was the only fly that truly represented the nymph form of the Western Salmon Fly. Cal Bird was a master fly tier and owned a small fly shop in San Francisco in the 1940 s and 50s. He also developed the Bird's Nest for the Truckee river. A little known fact that most tiers should know is that the dubbing loop tool was invented by Cal Bird.

OUR GRANDFATHERS' FLIES

BREADCRUST NYMPH

Originator – Rudy Sentiwany
Recipe:
Body: The brown quill from the butt of a dark brown saddle hackle. This quill must show distinct dark on the shiny side. The quill is flattened and wound to the shoulder
Thorax: Rusty brown fur dubbing
Hackle: Soft grizzly
Head: Black
Thread: Black
Hook: Down eye heavy wire nymph hook

David L. McElwain

Breadcrust Nymph

Step 1. Attach the thread to hook and advance to bend of hook.
Step 2. Tie in brown quill shiny side down and wrap forward bringing shiny side on top.
Step 3. Build thorax with dubbing.
Step 4. Tie in hackle in front of dubbing thorax.
Step 5. Palmer hackle 2-3 times pulling back between wraps and build head holding hackle back and whip finish.

By all indications the Breadcrust was a very controversial fly. My research indicates that its creator was Rudy Sentiwany. It seems that as soon as it was developed it began to undergo phases of change. Though it is still tied and fished today, the pattern is far different than the original.

Our Grandfathers' Flies

Blades' Olive Nymph

Originator – William Blades
Recipe:
Tail: Blue dun hackle fibers
Body: Golden olive seal fur – dubbing
Ribbing: Flat gold tinsel
Thorax: Olive seal fur dubbing
Wing case: Orange silk floss (4 strand floss)
Hackle: Honey badger
Thread: Yellow
Hook: Down eyed Nymph Hook

David L. McElwain

Blades' Olive Nymph

Step 1. Attach thread to hook and advance to bend in hook and tie in a section of hackle fibers for tail.
Step 2. Tie in the flat gold tinsel and lay back.
Step 3. Dub a 3" or so length of thread and wind forward to form body.
Step 4. Wind forward tinsel to segment body.
Step 5. Tie in a short section of orange 4 strand floss.
Step 6. Dub a short length of thread for thorax and build thorax.
Step 7. Stretch floss over top of thorax and tie off.
Step 8. Tie in hackle and make two palmers pulling down to form legs.

Blades, an Englishman and WWII veteran, moved to Chicago after the war. Bill Blades started teaching fly tying as recreation for servicemen. He taught tying to several hundred wounded marines at the Great Lakes Naval Hospital. It was discovered that the procedures used in tying flies aided these men to gain more use of their fine motor skills in their injured arms and hands, even with the crude artificial arms and hands of that era.

BLACK GNAT NYMPH

Originator: unknown
Recipe:
Body: Black Chenille
Hackle: Black
Wings: Grey quill
Thread: Black
Hook: Down eyed nymph hook

DAVID L. MCELWAIN

BLACK GNAT NYMPH

Step 1. Attach thread to hook and advance to bend of hook.

Step 2. Tie in a length of chenille and wrap forward leaving 3 times the length of eye at front of hook.

Step 3. Tie in hackle, palmering twice, pulling down and tying off.

Step 4. Select two sections of quill and pinch wrap into place leaving back measured to length of body.

Step 5. Build head and coat with lacquer or black hard head.

OUR GRANDFATHERS' FLIES

BEAVERKILL NYMPH

Originator: Judge James Fitch
circa 1880
Recipe:
Body: White floss
Ribbing: Brown silk
Tail: Brown Hackle barbules
Hackle Brown
Wings: Dark slate quill
Thread: Brown
Hook: Standard Sproat Nymph

David L. McElwain

Beaverkill Nymph

Step 1. Attach thread to hook, advance to bend, and tie in a section of hackle barbules.

Step 2. Tie in a length of brown silk and lay back.

Step 3. Tie in a length of white 4 strand floss and wrap forward creating body.

Step 4. Reverse wrap ribbing to hook eye.

Step 5. Select and tie in hackle and palmer 2 times pulling down and clipping off top.

Step 6. Select 2 sections of quill for wings, match and tie in, separating, build head and whip finish.

Our Grandfathers' Flies

Female Beaverkill Nymph

Originator: Judge James Fitch
circa 1880
Recipe:
Body: Muskrat fur dubbing with yellow chenille egg sac
Tail: Gray; Mallard
Hackle: Medium Red Brown
Wings: Gray Mallard
Head: Black

David L. McElwain

Female Beaverkill Nymph

Step 1. Attach thread to hook and advance to bend of hook.

Step 2. Tie in a section of Mallard flank.

Step 3. Tie in yellow chenille, make one wrap and tie off forming body

Step 4. Dub 3" of thread with muskrat fur, wrap forward toward hook eye forming body.

Step 5. Tie in Hackle and palmer one wrap pulling down and secure.

Step 6. Select two sections and quill and tie in (measure to length of hook) and secure.

Step 7. Build tapered head and whip finish and lacquer.

OUR GRANDFATHERS' FLIES

ATHERTON LIGHT NYMPH

Originator: John Atherton
circa 1951
Recipe:
Thread: Gray, dark brown or black
Hook: 3x long nymph hook 14-8
Tail: Three barbules of Wood Duck flank feather
Body: Natural seal fur
Rib: Oval gold tinsel
Thorax: 6 wraps of 15-20 size lead wire, cover lead will with thread
Wing cases: Two tiny eyes of the Jungle Cock feather
Hackle: Partridge

David L. McElwain

Atherton Light Nymph

Step 1. Attach thread to hook and advance to band of hook.
Step 2. Select 3 barbules of Wood Duck and secure with a single pinch wrap and splay with thumb to separate, continue by making to making two more thread wraps behind pinch wrap and secure.
Step 3. Tie in a length of oval gold tinsel and lay back.
Step 4. Dub 3" of thread and wrap forward to a little past center point of hook.
Step 5. Segment with gold tinsel, reverse wrap for better visibility.
Step 6. Tie in and wrap 6 times a length of lead wire or non lead wire – cover with a small amount of head cement and cover with thread while still wet.
Step 7. Tie in yarn and wrap forward to form thorax.
Step 8. Tie in hackle, palmer 2 times and clip off top.
Step 9. Tie in the Jungle Cock eyes separated by several wraps of thread.

Note: substitute for Jungle Cock is imitation or a small black feather with a smaller white tip, tied over top to keep them together – put a small drop of head cement between the feathers.

OUR GRANDFATHERS' FLIES

ATHERTON DARK NYMPH

Originator: John Atherton
circa 1951
Recipe:
Thread: Black 6/0
Hook: 3x long nymph hook
Tail: A few strands of cochy-bondhu hackle or dark furnace hackle barbules
Body: Muskrat or mole fur mixed with red-brown died seal dubbing
Note: gather all parts and mix in a coffee grinder or select reddish brown SLF dubbing.
Ribbing: Narrow (small) oval gold tinsel
Thorax: Same as body over 6 wraps of lead or non lead #20 - #15 wire
Wing Case: Bright blue feather from wing of Kingfisher
Hackle: Dark furnace or cochy-bondhu hackle

DAVID L. MCELWAIN

ATHERTON DARK NYMPH

Step 1: Attach thread to hook and advance to bend of hook, wrap and cover 6 wraps of #20 - #15 lead wire

Step 2. Tie in hackle barbules for tail.

Step 3. Tie in gold tinsel and lay back.

Step 4. Dub 3" or so of thread, wrap forward to create body.

Step 5. Bring forward the gold tinsel in reverse wraps.

Step 6. Dub 2" of thread from dubbing used for body and wrap forward.

Step 7. Tie in the hackle and make 2 palmers.

Step 8. Clip top of hackle off and cover with wing case feather.

Note: pick out dubbing of body between ribbing.

Note: A tip of a bright blue craft store feather will replace the Kingfisher feather tip.

THE ATHERTON #1

Wet Fly

Originator: John Atherton
circa 1951
Recipe:
Thread: Black
Hook: 20-10
Tail: Light cree hackle barbules
Ribbing: Narrow(small) oval gold tinsel
Body: A mixture of natural seal fur and dyed yellow seal fur or mohair
Hackle: Light cree
Wings: Brazilian mouse deer hair or the short speckled hairs at the base of a Fox squirrel tail
Note: a coffee grinder will mix the dubbing evenly. A substitute for body mix would be yellow-grey SLF dubbing.

DAVID L. McELWAIN

THE ATHERTON #1
Wet Fly

Step 1. Attach thread to hook and secure a section of hackle barbules for tail.

Step 2. Tie in oval gold tinsel and lay back.

Step 3. Dub a 3" length of thread and wrap forward, creating body.

Step 4. Reverse wrap gold tinsel segmenting body.

Step 5. Tie in wing hair over front of body.

Step 6. Tie in and palmer the hackle twice, push back with thread, whip finish and lacquer head.

Carrot Nymph

Originator: Ruben Cross
1898 -1958
Recipe:
Hook: Standard nymph hook
Thread: Black
Tail: Brown Hackle barbules
Body: Carrot colored floss silk
Thorax: Black chenille
Hackle: Soft dun
Head: Black

David L. McElwain

Carrot Nymph

Step 1. Attach thread to hook and advance to bend of hook, tie in hackle barbules for tail and secure.
Step 2. Tie in a length of floss and wrap forward creating body.
Step 3. Tie in a length of chenille and wrap to form thorax.
Step 4. Tie in a soft dun hackle and make 2 palmers, pulling back between wraps, tie off and whip finish.

Reuben Cross was lucky enough to grow up in the Neversink region of New York, the very same place Theodore Gordon spent endless hours along the banks. Reuben was one of the early 20th century "professional fly tiers and a classic Catskill style tier". He created some beautiful flies that collectors still value today. He was the creator of the "Cross Special" and the "Hair-winged Coachman", both dry flies. In 1936, Reuben authored "Tying American Trout Lures". He also wrote "Fur, Feathers and Steel", an off shoot of that book was pioneering the raising and breeding of roosters for select fly tying hackle.

OUR GRANDFATHERS' FLIES

GRAY GHOST

streamer

Originator: Carrie G. Stevens
1882 – 1970
Recipe:
Hook: Standard streamer hook 10-4
Thread: Black
Body: Orange floss
Ribbing: Flat silver tinsel
Wings: Golden Pheasant crest, four gray hackles
Tag: Flat silver tinsel
Throat: Golden Pheasant crest
Underbelly: Four to six strands of Peacock herl then white buck tail
Shoulders: A silver Pheasant body feather
Cheeks: Jungle Cock
Head: Black with orange band

DAVID L. MCELWAIN

GRAY GHOST
Streamer

Step 1. Start thread at bend of hook, tie in a length of tinsel and wrap tag, tie off and lay back.
Step 2. Tie in 4 strand floss and wrap to front of hook, segment body, with flat tinsel.
Step 3. Tie in Pheasant crest, then the wings over top.
Step 4. Then tie in Pheasant crest for throat.
Step 5. Rotate fly to expose bottom to tie underbelly.
Step 6. Tie in Peacock herl followed by white buck tail.
Step 7. Tie in the two shoulders on each side.
Step 8. Select a pair of Jungle Cock eyes for cheeks.
Note – cheeks can be made of artificial Jungle Cock or a black feather tip covered by a white feather tip.
Step 9. Whip finish and make head, start an orange floss segment on head then clear lacquer.

Carrie was self taught, but she created some of the most majestic and enduring steamers patterns ever designed. This Maine native developed dozens of patterns for land-locked salmon and giant brook trout located in Maine's Rangeley lakes region. Carrie's Gray Ghost, Blue Devil, Demon, Golden Witch and Orange Miller are now standards.

OUR GRANDFATHERS' FLIES

MORMON GIRL

Creator: Roy Donnelly
1940s
Recipe:
Hook: 9672 Mustad or equivalent wet fly hook size 4 through 10
Thread: Black 6/0
Tail: Golden Pheasant barbules
Rib: Embossed gold tinsel
Rear body: Red floss
Front body(thorax): Yellow chenille
Hackle: Soft grizzly
Wing: Badger guard hairs

David L. McElwain

Mormon Girl

Step 1. Attach thread to hook and advance to the bend of the hook.
Step 2. Tie in a section of Golden Pheasant barbules (measure tail to length of hook).
Step 3. Tie in flat gold tinsel and lay back, tie in red, 4 strand floss, generous length.
Step 4. Advance the floss forward to half the hook length.
Step 5. Reverse wrap the gold tinsel in even segments.
Step 6. Tie in the yellow chenille and wind forward to form the body or thorax.
Step 7. Tie in the hackle and palmer twice pulling back between wraps.
Step 8. Tie in the guard hair from the badger for the wing and splay slightly, build head and whip finish.

It seems that there was quite a crowd in the room when The Morman Girl was born. Bob Carmichael and Roy Donnelly were there in Jackson Hole Wyoming, of that we are certain. Carmichael had employed Donnelly to create this pattern. Jack Dennis remembers his grandfather using this fly and credits it as one of the most popular patterns.

Sofa Pillow

Originator: Pat Barnes
1907-1997
circa 1940s
Hook: Mustad 9672 or equivalent 4 – 10
Thread: Black 6/0
Tail: Dyed red goose quill section
Body: Red Floss
Wing: Red or gray squirrel tail
Hackle: Three or four brown saddle hackles

David L. McElwain

Sofa Pillow

Step 1. Attach thread to hook and advance to bend of hook
Step 2. Select a section of goose quill and using a pinch wrap secure the quill on top of the hook
Step 3. Tie in a length of 4 strand floss and wrap forward
Step 4. Select a moderate bunch of squirrel tail and measure just short of tail and tie in using a pinch wrap to secure the hair on top of hook
Step 5. Select the hackles of relative same length, tie in and palmer 4 to 6 times forward to hook eye, tie off and whip finish

Pat and his wife Sig, ran the premier fly shop and guide service in West Yellowstone, Montana for nearly 40 years. Pat learned to fish at an early age using grasshoppers and throughout his career he developed an impressive collection of Hopper patterns. Pat was a practical tier, he designed to catch fish. He tied the Sofa Pillow and the Jug Head that became must haves for successful fisherman during the early summer salmon fly hatches from the Big Hole in June to the Yellowstone river in August.

WOOLY WORM

Originator: unknown
Recipe:
Hook: Standard streamer 12-6
Thread: Black
Body: Black, brown, olive chenille
Tail: Red yarn or floss
Hackle: Grizzly
Note: color combinations can vary by tiers preferences.

David L. McElwain

Wooly Worm

Step 1. Attach thread and tie in red yarn or floss at bend of hook, add few wraps of lead covered by thread for weight.
Step 2. Tie in hackle at bend of hook.
Step 3. Tie in chenille and wrap to front of hook.
Step 4. Palmer hackle 6 -8 times to front of hook, whip finish.

Author – I included this fly in the collection because the first catch I made was with a wooly. When I was 3 or 4 years old my grandfather would put a wooly worm on the end of a cane pole and sit me down on the banks of the stream at Bennett Springs State Park in Missouri. It just represents the beginning of a fascination and passionate relationship between me and trout.

Biography

David Lee McElwain spent his early years in Marshfield, Missouri. He was introduced to fishing at a very early age. It only took him a few years to discover a local trout fishery located a few miles from his farm.

Special weekends were spent at Bennett Springs State Park with his grandfather, father and uncles, aunts and cousins. He learned the art of slow jigging for trout with a cane pole and a wooly worm . His 12th birthday gift determined his travels and adventures for most of his life. The introduction of the Zebco 202 Combo Pack was "just the ticket".

He mastered farm pond bass and catfish whenever he could sneak away from the family's dairy farm. Once he was old enough to provide his own transportation, David started fishing the cold trout streams of Bennett and other trout fisheries in the area.

Every day after work you could find him by the a stream slow gigging and watching several fly fisherman applying their skill. One day, while passing a yard sale he spotted several long rods leaned up against a saw horse. There was a yellow fiberglass fly rod with a reel and line for the price of $10.00.

This was his first fly rod made by Eagle Claw a 6/7 wt two piece rod. The owner had assured him would be" just the ticket "to learn fly fishing. Well, it was not as easy as the owner had assured him would be. Every day, after work, you would find him standing on the side of the stream, watching the fly fisherman and casting. It took about two weeks before he was able to actually catch a fish with his new rod and novice skill.

One day one of the fly fisherman wandered down the stream and offered a bit of instruction. A friendship that was to last 30 plus years began that day. Charlie Reading taught him to cast and tie flies. The skills he learned that summer from Charlie he honed over the years. Through his business career and other endeavors he was always   not too far from a stream where he could practice his skills which soon became flawless.

Today, you can find him fishing the streams of the Rocky mountains. He is a certified Adaptive Fly Fishing Practitioner and keeps himself busy fulfilling numerous invitations for fly tying exhibitions. He shares his gift of teaching with the likes of the Wounded Warriors and Wish of a Lifetime Foundation. He is a member of Trout Unlimited, The Federation of Fly Fishers, Adaptive Fly Fishing Association and The Fly Dressers Guild.

BIBLIOGRAPHY

"The Complete Fly Fisherman: The Notes and Letters of Theodore Gordon" edited by John McDonald, 1947

Preston Jennings, "A Book of Trout Flies" 1935

"W.C.Dette Dry Flies" catalogue 1935

John Atherton, "The Fly and the Fish" 1951

Informational sites for on-line research
    fishingmuseum.org.uk
    catskillflytyersguild.org
    americanmuseumofflyfidhing.com
    classictrout.com
    detteflies.com

www.ingramcontent.com/pod-product-compliance
Lightning Source LLC
Chambersburg PA
CBHW041551220426
43666CB00002B/39